Renée Ashley's
THE
REVISIONIST'S DREAM

"In the end, you are everything," says THE REVISIONIST'S DREAM, "tree, mountain, fish/ in the mirrored stream, blue heart/ pounding like a fist in the chest." Renée Ashley is fascinated by the strange shapes and stranger stories desire, for minutes or forever, makes of us. She easily manages the cosmic scale, from the head voice of prophetic authority through the middle tones of spousal intimacy, tender and resentful, all the way down to the large-eyed silence of dogs, so often her symbol of the blunt, impenetrable life that, snuffling around our feet, knows, even when we don't, that we belong to it. With her archaic purity and simplicity, her silvery poise and steely resolve, Ashley is an angel just a little too shrewd and gutsy and heartbroken to belong in heaven. She's a poet, that is, and she brings us a book of such wisdom and work and passion that we call it a vision.

—James Richardson
author of *How Things Are, As If,* and
Vectors: Five Hundred Aphorisms

Renée Ashley transforms ancient myths and invents modern allegories. Here is a poetry that is elemental, hypnotic and sonorous. Like a jeweler examining a stone for the quality of the cut, the consistency and color of brilliance, in poem after poem, we feel an intense and wise scrutiny, and witness an intelligence that infuses the object of its gaze with possibilities, and then, to dazzling effect, varies and multiplies perspectives. Here are chord-changing boleros of the psyche and heart and dreamscapes where nothing ever stands still and "the story changes all the time."

—Gray Jacobik
author of *The Double Task* and
The Surface of Last Scattering

Ms Ashley reminds us with a sweet succinctness that originality has to do with what is very old, with origins indeed, in order to have much truck with the New—always a doubtful proposition. The dreams she attributes to her Revisionist are indeed the ordering of ancient visions, made new with a full heart, a clear mind.

—Richard Howard
itzer Prize-winning author of eleven
umes of poetry including *Trappings:*
w Poems

Books by Renée Ashley

Salt
Winner of Brittingham Prize in Poetry
University of Wisconsin Press

The Various Reasons Of Light
Avocet Press Inc

THE
REVISIONIST'S DREAM

poems

Renée Ashley

Avocet Press Inc   New York

AVOCET PRESS

Published by
Avocet Press Inc
19 Paul Court, Pearl River, NY 10965
http://www.avocetpress.com
books@avocetpress.com

Copyright © 2001 by Renée Ashley

Library of Congress Cataloging-in-Publication Data

Ashley, Renée.
  The revisionist's dream / by Renée Ashley.
      p. cm.
  ISBN 0-9705049-2-6
  I. Title.
  PS3551.S387 R4 2001
  811'.54—dc21

                          2001001348

Printed in the USA
First Edition

Cover Design: Melanie Kershaw

for Jack
and to Dr. Richard Bratset
and
Dr. Richard Wiseman
who told me

and for Carmen Jones

The universe is made of stories, not of atoms.
—Muriel Rukeyser

ACKNOWLEDGMENTS

The American Literary Review: "Sometimes the Wheel Is on Fire"

The American Voice: "That Fall: Icarus in the Exurbs," "Nemesis," and "The Weaving: Her Voice (Another Poem about Penelope)"

The Antioch Review: "On the Death of Proteus"

Barrow Street: "Drown"

Black Swan Review: "Apostrophe" and "With the Forest Just Beginning"

Chelsea: "Letter to a Husband"

Clay Palm Review: "First Book of the Moon" (reprint)

The Harvard Review: "Arethusa, Deep"

Indiana Review: "Some Demeter"

The Kenyon Review: "The Revisionist's Dream *(I)*" and "The Revisionist's Dream *(III)*"

The Literary Review: "First Book of the Moon"

Notre Dame Review: "Some Other Woman Speaks to Elpenor after His Fall from Circe's Roof" and "*Prologue* to First Book of the Moon"

Poet Lore: "The Embers, the Light"

Poetry: "A Sort of a Love Poem"

Southern Poetry Review: "Lost Dogs," "The Language of Sirens (To a Father)," and "Nostos: Not a Retelling at All"

Sycamore Review: "What She Wanted" and "What We Don't Understand"

"Lost Dogs" appears in *Dog Music*, from St. Martin's Press, edited by Joseph Duemer and Jim Simmerman, 1996.
"On the Death of Proteus" appears in *Winners: A Retrospective of the Washington Prize*, 1999.

The author wishes to express her gratitude to the MacDowell Colony for time and hospitality.

TABLE OF CONTENTS

A selection from "First Book of the Moon" has been chosen by the artist Larry Kirkland to be etched into the marble walls in the main concourse of the rebuilt Penn Station Terminal in Manhattan.

We dream our lives but the rivers breathe flint and spark
and, each night, we believe in everything—the shifting edge of light
and dark, the possibility of what we think we are, and what we think
    we see.

—Variant Moon: Eclipse
(Moon as Abstraction)

I

THE REVISIONIST'S DREAM *(I)*

Old as seawater. And the dream as large as a sea.
We dream like that. And longer than that. Wider.
And hear the sound of bleak bells like flat stone
on flat stone. We stand — our hands are empty
and the floor is steep, the floor is a deep sea
with fish like stones who call like bells. Like
brittle bells. And the song is running water.
And the water is rising.

And the prison we choose
is narrow, and we swear we never dreamed those walls.
So the way the light breaks out from the night
is how we break away, how we carry our lives
like a sack or a sadness — and we are merely river;
the water is sweet is shallow is slow but the dream
is dark and smoky, like a woman's hair let down.
It winds like that.

WHAT SHE WANTED

A sudden blow: the great wings beating still....
            —Yeats, "Leda and the Swan"

Not what you think. She imagined
love, yes, and the wings thrashing

with the force of it, white feathers,
white water, flashing all around,

and the breath at her neck, like a blade's
keen side, one edge of his shameless

desire. And hers, she will tell you,
like a deft honing in cool water. She wanted him

like that. And she wanted him to risk
any small thing — his life, for instance,

if that were possible — to possess her.
She wanted him to traverse oceans, cross

silver bodies of perilous water; she wanted
him reflected there, and vulnerable — blind

to all but fierce need and the brave wind
teasing her hair; she wanted him unaware of wave

and precipitous rock. And she liked the word
tread, the idea of the watery fuck —

the cool shade at the steep, muddy banks,
and the current in between. She wanted him

to own all that: the depths of need
and the body's fallible knowledge.

How far one might go for love,
and the waters one crosses to get there.

ARETHUSA, DEEP

Fear and the heart streaming like rain —
then the quick drop to foil love. How,
in the earth's heart, you are changed.
How you emerge knowing how to fall,
how to rise again. And all the while,
love's divided tongue calling your name.

NEMESIS

*[Nemesis] leaped ashore, and transformed
herself into this wild beast or that, but could not
shake Zeus off, because he borrowed the form of
even fiercer and swifter beasts.*
—Robert Graves, *The Greek Myths*

What we are not and might be: each day
we show ourselves: tree, mountain, fish

in the mirrored stream, blue heart
pounding like a fist in the chest.

We are nothing we know for long.
And little is certain but the onslaught

of desire. The gods take expedient form,
descend and turn to fast-running dreams.

And beauty is the least of love. We bare
our fear or not. Either way, one god in his hunger

wants her: she flees in her silver skin,
sleek in the rapid water. Behind her

the god called *fast,* called *cruel*,
swims in a seal's thick fur. What we fear,

what we argue against, *is* love — what changes
is the open eye, the urgent, insatiable heaven.

SOME DEMETER

I sing about Demeter and
her daughter, Persephone, whom
Hades snatched away....
—Homeric Hymn to Demeter (II)

I

Today the old
woman is gray

     and hard; she is a stone falling;

she bends into
the darkness; she

     cannot conceive of not moving downward, cannot

imagine an end
to the unname-

     able depth. She's concerned about time, about how

much must pass
before she moves

     beyond falling, arrives, hits the bottom, if you will, or
       whether,

in that wry way
that is the only

      way, there is no bottom. She considers:

she could fall endlessly
(she'd miss her bus home,

      the dog would go hungry. She is concerned

about hunger. And
dogs. And falling.)

      She is concerned about time and its ram-

ifications. And she's
waiting to find out who

      she might be and what she will know when it ends.

II

Or, the old woman
is a queen; she's gold

      and red. She's ermine. She's been having

these dreams: of darkness,
of stones. She dreams

      of deep water running, dark as black shadow;

or she dreams of no
water. (She's missed

      her bus; the dog is hungry.) Time falls like the hooves

of horses. She has been
remiss: the girl is gone

      again, and the sorrow is as dull as gray stone.

Or she dreams
the daughter:

      the color of plums, the color of berries,

of red seeds. She dreams
the dark man, the chariot

      rising and falling, dreams horses like black shadows,

like black fire — the wheels
are like suns, his hands fast

      as flames, his body like the weight of an earth.

She dreams sorrow
the color of horses,

      a reign over nothing. The sky is the color of ash.

III

Or the whole sky dreams
the girl, the man,

>   and the woman is truly gold; she is the ground waving, she
>   bends

at the waist, her plain hands
rich with black dirt. The girl

>   would go home; the man beneath her — his chthonic body
>   like a dark seed,

like a great stone
the color of shade —

>   stands in a shadow the color of horses. (The dog is ripe

with waiting; hunger
is fast water, the color

>   of bright sun.) And the woman is as wild as grass.

And time is a vast meadow
which opens beneath her feet

>   and into which our precarious sky falls like a steady rain.

THE WEAVING: HER VOICE
(Another Poem About Penelope)

How little I understand! at best, the rhythm of the dependable sun
    on the flinty water, the weaving
of the steady moon amidst the waves — yes, and time like a shower
    of arrows. The sea
changes. But what makes men wander? Neither unspent lust nor lack
    of love! Ripe with rumor, men
crawl, promise laid out behind them like slime behind slugs, penises
    tucked in their dark places
like bags of wine or salted meat slung below deck — and off they go,
    the swine. Tell
me — what dreams must they run from? what can they be thinking
    of? Not wives. Not sons.

Even long before the boy was born, his father's eyes cast out to sea,
    and our shared sun
strung ribbons of light on its surface, threw them down on the waves,
    wove
the sticky net. And he watched it like a blind man watching — no
    telling
what he imagined there, or what his weak gods showed him. I looked
    too, and saw the sea —
just that. Water and light, in depths like barrows. Idiocy in honor's
    guise: to displace
lovers, fathers — Bah! We are not fishes, not fishes' wives. The
    sea's no place for men

at all! But husbands are such royal asses. They can't just look. Oh,
those women
are no secret. And I'm no fool. I'm a pretty wild ride myself, and still
those liaisons
suck him merrily downstream. He comes back. I take no pride in that.
It's commonplace.
But, still, it's the wives that rate a crown: insufferable weaving,
the waiting like thirst, the ravenous welcome with the dog looking on.
Oh, I can foresee
all that: a beggar's disguise, the long fires of the greedy dead, some
tell-

tale music in the emptied hall. Why else would I wait? Some hearts
bear witness and never tell
a soul! We are the ships our husbands should cling to! Our tongues
are the omens
those men should heed: there is nothing beyond their dreadful sea
but more sea. They're shirkers and stinkers! And what can we tell
their sons?
that we stay home? wear our long hair up — and wait? that we bind
the strands tightly, weave
them into the dull pattern of our days? Not likely. The mind of a man
is the dwelling place

of mystery. No answers there: they're moved by gods, for heaven's
sake! Place
your ear here, in the curve of this breast — hear the whisper? That
tells
more than seaborne men can ever know. It's the patient heart that
weaves
the miracle, not the sunstruck or the loveless. Tell your sons that!
What men-
dacity to blame the gods! What cowardice! We build our own
prisons.
We make the choices that bend us at the knee. If we wear crowns of
sea-

wrack, it's by choice. Such monsters we create! Men drown in a sea
they fill themselves! It's the heart that is the sturdy god. I place
my faith on dry land, then deep in the body. This I'm sure of: it's
    treason
otherwise. And sacrifice: men pay huge ransoms for their salty lives,
    then tell
tales, justify their grief with piddling joy, return, spread their semen
thick in the furrows of their wives and assume we've

borne, with grace, their absent seasons — as if we were mere baga-
    telles to barter
for cocks and cravings! Such ill-placed hope! No acumen at all!
    Dead men
see more: the risk, the thousand threads of poison woven in persis-
    tent hearts, unraveled.

SOME OTHER WOMAN SPEAKS TO ELPENOR AFTER HIS FALL FROM CIRCE'S ROOF

Youngest, least done with your days, you fell
ballast-heavy past the windows of those rungs,
such a slender ladder as your life — all

that falling and the knot of your neck undone.
In the swinish yard, the remnants of long drink
wasted and the body of a boy who had a taste

for the stars; the men were off again, their own
descent joyless before them. The pale dust settled
and you, too, were gone. And all because some woman

loved a man! I say I dream you again, raise you up,
say that gravity with its perfect eyesight does not
see you, that your own weight is nothing, that you

do not struggle like a boy falling, but remain
passive in the air with your stars. No contrivance
is beyond love. You must listen: we can make

a comely magic now — in this dream you are falling
but timeless. Trust me: do not look down, not once.
Don't think of gods or of fate with its nasty

smile; don't think of men: they leave you. Don't imagine
the meaningless heft of your body dropping like rain
or the wide, insatiable hips of the earth rising to meet you.

II

THE REVISIONIST'S DREAM *(II)*

She dreamed and the dream was of language. She dreamt
words had yellow wings, had a thousand delicate fingers,
had big tusks, had balls — that their mutable voices rose
from some distance and carried to her on a blue wind. No.
She dreamed of water. She dreamed of a single bright leaf
tangled in a dark stream. She did. But you can't take

her literally, and the story changes all the time. Take
the time she told you about the memory: that she dreamt
the whole world was memory, and that the recollection of leaving
was really a leaving again, was motion itself like a dream, light-
    fingered,
light-footed. That leaving was blue and red, had wings but had no
dreams of its own. And memory like that — like getting up, rising

from a favorite chair, your legs working, your body rising
with no more thought than the dream taking off from sleep. But she's
    taken
some liberties; after all, it's her dream — she's dreaming it — and she
    knows
the dream itself knows nothing. The story changes all the time, yet
    the dreams
seem true enough — but truth is a fitful thing, time is quick-fingered
and slick; and she thinks time does have wings and is the color of
    truth. She believes

in at least a million truths and in time sweeping them into a heap like
    leaves.
She believes that most of all. And she's certain that new dreams rise
from the gathering, use their wings like fingertips,
like the dead waking and, somewhere between rest and will, taking
up their touch again. But no, it's foolish to believe her. Her dreams
are pale language — but there's still the sky, the white, nomadic

clouds, their silhouettes against the blue, their histories, what

nobody
expects of heaven. No: it's different. The dream is exactly the size of
   her life. And ordinary. It leaves
the enormous and abstract aside, calls up the hard, black, dreamy
streets and the dark smell of tar. Calls up the good white dog, brings
   back the wild rose
streaming up the dogwood like ribbons and flowering in the air. And
   language like that, taking
advantage of what truth leaves behind. But it's hard to put your
   finger

on it, because the story changes all the time — the dream is light-
   fingered.
But the colors are true: the yellow light rising, not on the blue wind,
   but as if yellow could know
what it takes to rise. As if yellow had dreams. And language like
   that, too, always taking
the borrowed shape of time, the coming and going, a cloudy promise
   crossing bright water; the leaves
on the other side shimmer in the wind. But the story changes like the
   wind and now a red bird rises
at the dreamer's feet, a great heart, and beats the blue air; the heart
   dreams

of language flying, it batters the air like fingers drumming, one word
   leaving
off, the next swept up on the arc of an innocent wing. And, risen,
the heart takes direction and the dreamer is lost — yes, unimportant
   — deep in the language and dream.

FIRST BOOK OF THE MOON

*And God made two great lights; the greater
light to rule the day, and the lesser light to
rule the night....*
        —Genesis 1:16

Prologue

i

When the moon first burst out, when the bodies became two, sun
and moon, we held up a stone to measure that new breadth, that
        arguable depth;
and we spoke in murmurs shallow as veins: the beginnings of the
        bright
tongue, a confluence of magics, whisper like opal, like a trickle of
        quartz, and the whole body listening,
the whole sky. And when the moon, by itself, shone on the lip of the
        oyster, on the spire
of the conch, we thought: glass in the eye, fire in the sand. We said:
byss and abyss, nothing and all. It was moon like a brittle saucer,
        like
a severed pearl. It was bigger than us and it had ideas; we heard it
        sighing.
And the dark, too, with its big ears, heard the whisper, the white
        breath
hanging overhead, the long road throwing its broken shadow, the
        sliver of light
between. We were all restless, lunatic, and stunned. We had found
        the moon
in the midst of a night thick with black sky. We praised its shallow
        lisping;
we dreamed its center: we gave it a heartbeat and its dense white
        bone.

And after we built the moon in our dream, there was more moon: an
    eyelid fattening
in the dark. And so we reinvented seeing, and light, like a somber,
    slow insight,
hung there in the sky, its smile askew. We could have held it in our
    hands.
And around us, our landscape grew wings: depth flew up like a wild
    bird, shadows
eased past the edge of the mountain, descended at the canyon's
    irregular rim. Night
was a shadow then. We could walk through it, and we were changed.
    And, still, bright fish
leaped from the black water, the river ran — but now those fish were
    silver moons
and the river wore moon ribbons, bright moon beads, scarves of the
    filmiest moon. There was no going
back. The hollow in our cupped hands waited for the moon; lips, at
    the cusp of daylight
and dusk, were shaped to cradle it: the breathy *ahhh* in the waiting,
the tongue at rest, low in the mouth, ready for the new light to settle
    there, and remain.

New Moon
(Moon as Utterance)

I can't remember the first time we said *moon.* We were lightheaded by
      then,
dizzy: moon-drunk. And then it was gone — the oddest thing, the
      new moon,
no moon at all, that slipping back and stunned again, and absence
      vast as a sun,
vaster, and everyone naked as fish in the black room of our dream.
      We spoke
in whispers. We crawled on our bellies through that hollow vowel
      as if
we believed we could breathe there, as though our whole lives were
      suspended,
flickering sparks in its long, dank length. There was no horizon, no
      edge to cut
the shadow away. We were bereft, less than lightless. We said it
      again, softly:
m-o-o-n, drew it out like a supple river; it echoed in a valley we could
      not see —
we had lost the moon! And, for that moment, we were voiceless with
      sorrow:
no moon to lift our impenetrable night, no breath of light beneath.
And the gaping mouth of our dream drank us in; we were moving
through the dark. We missed what we had become, what we'd
      seemed alongside
the extravagant light; we took its shape, we carried that absent moon
      on our backs
and we mourned: moon like a longing, terrible as a god. Moon the
      color of ivory, lit by flame.
Moon the color of palest flesh. Of absolution. Moon capable of
      setting the mountain on fire.
Moon as the blessing, gone now — that light by which we could not
      see. We cried: *moon.*

II

Increscent Moon
(Moon as Incantation)

Nothing ever stood still: the black wind unsettled the absolute night,
and the dreamed moon stuttered. Its window of light swung open;
    the timorous rind
followed on the great bronze rump of the sun — antiphons of light
    and light —
and the white heartbeat carried us on its back, memory like a pulse,
    the leaping
river in our veins. Anticipation was silver fish at our throats; and
    hope
had its own rhythm. The crevice moon slid behind the feathery fir,
    beyond
branches like shadowy, many-winged birds, and dangled its thread of
    light
in that black ocean, the sky. We watched the dark play against the
    pale,
thin stream, urged the light to take on more; we sang its name over,
    sang
in bright waves, driven by the moon — moon barely there, a rent in
    the sky,
and then the moon unfurled: meniscus, half-eye, moon like a fist —
and the white mask turned toward us, its silhouette sharp as chipped
    horn,
its face like a dream of rough water. And it sang, descant, then out of
    control,
moon of a music we could not understand. It flooded the sky and we
    swam
in the pool of it, swam the moon spilling over, the length of it, the
    breadth,
moon in furious proportion, unfettered by songs we might sing. And
    when our feet

found the earth again, when we bent to the water to scoop up the
  moon,
it would not be contained. Moon of its own accord, we were nothing
  to it.
The woodlands flew apart, beat a thousand shades of dark against
  the sky,
and the waters ran like a dream of hope, fast, and white with the
  weightless moon,
bright as a burnished heaven until our shadows passed over.

III

Variant Moon: Eclipse
(Moon as Abstraction)

We must have closed our eyes. Something in the steep sky changed:
    the night
held its breath and a perfect black ate the moon. It moved like a
    whisper,
slow as a sigh; we didn't want to see it. But the whole sky stood still
while the moon gave in, while the darkest dark cast itself over the
    light.
And we waited and listened for the stopped heart of the moon
but it did not come. Its great eye closed; the precise dark slid
from the farther side, and it was gone — what moon shone down?
We were small lives, poised in the dark. And what was bright
had shrewd claws. But brilliant birds sang deep in the unyielding
trees; the sky was glass and slick as fast water. All these things
converged: what danced on the surface, what burrowed in the bone,
was mystery. We dream our lives. But the rivers breathe flint and
    spark
and, each night, we believe in everything — the shifting edge of light
and dark, the possibility of what we think we are, and what we think
    we see.

IV

Decrescent Moon
(Moon as Hypothesis)

And the whole world slows down. The moon exhales, breath like a
    bartering,
like a blowing away: moon in the past tense — what we have lived.
And light like a coin spent. This is the way absence is conjugated:
    the dark's
empty fist, its blind eye, the giving of night back to the night.
We peel it back like a skin and where there is black we imagine
white; we are the keepers of black and of white. And we are nothing.
And where there is shadow, we rise like the stream over bones, we
    cover
the canyon with singing the color of moons — even in the dark, some
    birds
wrestle with the idea of song. We are entire and seldom certain. And
    within the canyon
is another canyon. And a sky. The world is shortsighted. We speak
the language of tongues and fire. We speak ivory and deep water.
    This throbbing
is the shape of expectation. And our hope is imperfect. We hear the
    present
like a whisper, like a rustle of bright fish in a night-colored
stream, like a breathing deep in sleep. We carry the past like broken
    glass.
We call it *moon*. What we have learned. And the heart is an obliga-
    tion, is a bird
with dark wings, is a dream; we take with us its watery echo, at the
    bend
of our wrists, at our uncovered throats, visible as the landscape
    itself,
as the river beneath the changeable moon, and the mountains, the
    deepening chasms
which the black sky leans towards and lights with anticipated fire.

WITH THE FOREST JUST BEGINNING

All poems begin like this: the difficult
half-light, the trees a faint outline in the sand.

But somewhere there'll be a white gate, waist-
high and latched, and a first pale bird who'll

arrive and make thread-like tracks across the un-
embellished land; no one will know he's come.

And the vague sun might glide up from its depth
unnoticed, and the light just might seep

over the edge of the quiet, nearly-visible
mountains; a cluster of cedar or willow or pine

might be drawn upward before you — but slowly,
slowly. And then, if you're lucky, something small

and quick-footed will slip from the low scrub
and scatter the untouched soil. The bird will become

an instant of fierce color deep back on a branch.
And the gate might shift, the latch

lift up. The grasses may quicken around you, and,
as you begin to perceive your place at the edge

of the tentative wood, you might pick out the small
yellow eye in the gold field beside you, might catch

the white stream's unfaltering voice in the trees, the timber
of that singular forest rising from indistinct ground.

LOST DOGS

Sweetheart,
        The fog is pudding-thick and the lost
dog, the black one we coaxed home from the park, is wild with
    unhappiness (no
one calls him sweetheart). He hoisted his withered leg
and pissed circles like smoke rings on the sofa; he was howling, I
    swear, "I'll be Home
for Christmas." Some sort of miserable miracle. But that's how
    it is here.
Anyway, we've got to stop stealing lost dogs. It makes them
    melancholy

and, besides, the house is getting smaller all the time. Melancholy
seems the rule now. How long *have* you been gone? The lost
dog, the grey one, has come home; I'd figured he was dead but here
he sits, riddled with bootjack, steamy with wanderlust. He may just
    know
by heart, now, the scent of comfort, these mild fires that burn at
    home.
Remember your last departure? Remember the final leg

of your already too-long journey? The blind hound who'd lost his
    leg
to the snowplow had left us all cold and melancholic —
the bad news hit you hard. The dog healed, but you were home-
sick to begin with and, back then, anguish was the face we wore for
    everything we lost.
But the dog still hobbles the rock ledge; sightless, three-legged, he
    doesn't know
he's a candidate for sorrow. There's a tricky lesson here:

something about grace or humor, something about the here-
and-now. About patience. You see, it's all in the understanding:
       legs,
it would seem, aren't the issue. No,
I think it's absence, and how, because we're only human, we give in
       to melancholy.
It's about how loneliness and sorrow set the soul loose
to seek what it still can't seem to find at home.

Well, we just keep waiting for some word, hoping these notes find
       you heading home-
ward. I tell the dogs you're coming, you're needed, you'll be here
soon. Did I tell you about the strange one with the ragged ear who,
       obviously, was lost
and hungry, not hurt, but tired, worn out from his wandering? By the
       time he got here his legs
were shaky and the pads of his feet were raw. For two days he slept;
       he seemed sort of melancholy
when he woke but, then, suddenly, he up and ran off with the grizzled
       pup from down below. No

one's seen them for a week now. The man who kept the grizzled one
       doesn't seem to know
he's gone. I keep driving around the lake, but the dogs aren't there;
       perhaps they've found a home.
I'm trying not to think about it. I worry about the ones who go, and I
       get melancholy.
It's the fog, I think, that makes me so sad. It's difficult to see clearly
       here.
Between the mist and the low stone fences, we're lucky we don't
       break a leg
just taking the short hike to the main road for mail. We've lost

the knack of the smooth stroll. No, we're too aware that here
and there trouble hangs thick as this home-grown fog — and we
       don't need a leg-
up on blindness or melancholy. No, Sweetheart, we stay home to
       keep from getting lost.

A SORT OF A LOVE POEM

The way all poems
   are love poems, this
is a love poem. What

is love anyway? and what
   makes the lover's
assent different from

an unenraptured, "Yes,
   I'll have more
coffee" or "Yes, trash

is collected Thursdays"
   — what is Thursday
anyway? A day after

another, the way love,
   its sequential heart
bursting, follows on

another love, or
   the way two loves
might follow on two

more. This is the way
   all poems are love
poems: one thing

abutting the next,
   one word, one
love, then one angle

of particular light
   descending
on the unsettled water,

the hand in a hand,
   and the head nodding
yes — that light

and how it makes us
   feel, how we
do, so unwittingly, nod,

how we seem to see
   so clearly
after the light is gone.

DROWN

No rain but
Black glass for
Sky the quick
Darkening
That cold silk
All around!
And my breath
Like perfect
Black pearls rising

NOSTOS: Not A Retelling At All

And when long years and seasons wheeling
brought around that point of time ordained
for him to make his passage homeward....
—Robert Fitzgerald, translator,
The Odyssey

Oh, god, the invocation! Yes!
Let's begin!
Not the tale itself, not here, but the admonition!
The hastening. Now, that's consequential —
Let's give him that! He's grown too fat
On waves; he's still midstream. And wavering.
Muse, set the good fire, get a strong draught rising —
Help me spend a juicy haunch or two.
Summon your father, please! Let's coax *him* out:
He's castaway himself — by default!
This mortal's dallied many years too long;
There's more to do. Let's send him home —
And, beyond the poem's consequence, make song.

So, set the scene: the shimmery edge of the endless
Sea, the stern shore like a night sky or like dark
Laughter, the one bright bird on the lip
Of swell and strand
— white as a crying out
as the blaze in the eye
of a furious sun —
And the wave, the open mouth
Of the water,
Beckoning.

i

Imagine this: bird like an anger, anger like a wing
  — You, of the son, of the fabric of wife, Go home.
Drag your wishful bones over the boiling sea
  To the shallows that wear your name: Absence
And Self like an inverse sky, like deep water
  Or a violent storm. The wine is still strong;
You are beautiful and mean. You are old.
  And you have been gone too long: there are men
Who wear your absence like extravagant charms —
  They are eating your moony-eyed cattle, drinking
Your stores of blood-red wine. They beleaguer
  Your wife, would take her in hand and in deed,
But she is cautious and strong: she is the keeper
  Of your bed and your name, of your homeland,
And your coming home. She weaves your hours. Listen:
  From the rock where you weigh your misfortune,
You can hear the breathy swing of thread against thread,
  The shuttle of her sigh. She is waiting, but weary
With waiting; she is taut with love, and she has slept
  Alone. You have lain with witches and whores: your goddess
Is a sun and you rise and fall with her; she weaves, as well —
  A finer cloth, and brighter. But nothing there is real:
She would give you forever, eat you like bread. And now
  She is out-ranked and pitiful: watch for wings, for the coming
And going. Change is crossing the stubborn water.
  The passage is gold in your palm. You will earn it —
It is what you believe you have yearned for. Go home.

ii

But first, tell the secret: you know fear like a consort, like
A pulse, your marrow, a wing rising against the white stem
Of the body, the long bone like an arrow — horn, ivory,
Tusk — a wind in the spine, the eye of the heart: that gist
Where the known fear burrows. And you are right
To be afraid: your own shortcomings and the anger of gods
Pursue you. You have been haughty; you claimed your grief.
And the horizon is still your passion; the past, your ballast
And hope: you wear it like an old wound. But you have never
    balked;
You are sung and you are lost. Heroes are made from envy,
    Not return; they're strung like a bow with whispers
And the long apostrophe of wind at their sails. Tell the story!
    Give the rhapsode a glimmer of the fairer truth, then
The fateful sailing. Lend him your deepest tale, the one
    Nearest candor: the deft poverty of the body alone,
The abject rag of the carcass railing at the edge of the difficult
    Sea, a tide of sorrow beneath that cicatrix moon. Help him
Tune the drum of your heart — as it rattles the white bone,
    As it calls up the dogged, importunate eye of what matters most
        in your life.

Now, recall: your days are filled with minor gods and men
  Who wear gods' clothes: so you swallowed the wind.
The silver wire was your undoing, and your sadness
  Followed like rain. No words could wash you back
Again; you wore bleak robes, smelled of olive wood
  And brine. You thought the wing of your heart
Would break. And the daylight was not your friend:
  Your eyes burned, your skin was a desert. Your mouth
Was full of salt, and the birds knew you were reeling.
  Cattle lowed on the spit. And everyone forgets
Something. But nothing warmed you like the woman missing,
  The hollow hammer of the heart, loneliness, that cavern
Of long nights. Hunger like a wind. But the sea
  Is still angry. You are not home yet. And nothing
Is the dish you are served! Trust this: what makes us beautiful
  Makes us mean. You are a trickster and a braggart:
You are a man — and willful. Wily enough to extinguish
  The giant's eye, to ride from the hopeless cave
At the belly of the favored white ram, all that way to the
    rock's hard mouth
  And into the maniac light. To the cusp of the deep and
    spiteful sea.
You are a fool and a liar. You love your wiles more
  Than your wife; you bartered her long years, her sorrow —
That woman's tale — for idiot pride. Granted: you are the victim
    of sun
  And sorceress, monsters and sea-vamps whose voices have risen
Like a cold edge beneath you. Given: your petulant gods
  Shook you like dice. Prodigal father, husband
To no one, who is at fault? Ponder your spirit,
  Your fervor, your flaws.... Your gods are cast
In the likeness of men. *Of men!*
  And men's weaknesses plague them.

iv

And then there is that absolute truth, truth
    Like a star or a moon, like a wing or a shimmering
Flame. You had to hear it from the dead: all around you
    Your world is dying, and shade by shade
They told you so. There isn't much time;
    Shadow is descending on us all.
The tales were clear — they were adamant: even
    The dead believe in living. They wear
Their torn skins like long rumors; you
    Take them on and they swirl at your feet
Like smoke. They spread the stories
    That make their own lives true: we know
Ourselves by history. We wear it, visible
    As ragged flesh, the tally of unremarkable
Lives. Look further, beyond the precise fire
    Burning like darkness around you.
Ignore your own fear: we are all
    Drawn to the same flames, the same
Seas — wave after wave of our lives,
    The fire and swell, and all the long nights
Rowing. And everything depends on the scars.
    The dead will always bring us home.
And the sea will always throb
    Like your own poor blood pounding;
And dawn will come with its bright wings
    And you will journey, always, to and across
The same grave bodies of water. You will go home.
    You'll come to familiar sand and the dog
Will know you: you are the bone of his dreams.
    He will see you, the brass light on the dread-
Colored ocean, the lift of the candescent waves,
    Their surfaces purled with bright fish
And longing. You are the arc of his overdue sun.

Rest there. Let him catch the scent
Of your sea rags. Before he dies, know:
You are his wide ocean, his patchwork wind,
The moon in its silver cup. And, then, beyond
  His death, the others: you are the man
Washed up, finally ashore, a tranquil sea
  Behind him. And men will oppose you,
Will die in violent waves in your hall:
  Always one war, or another! Your courage
Will be reckoned by the changeable gods.
  And you will lie with your wife in the long
Tangle of night; and until you die,
  The sea will call out your name, and you will
Answer. And then, from the profound water,
  From the source of your heartbreak, a peaceful
Death, passage like an absence of sorrow,
  The wing of your breath departing
Like a long wound healed.

V

Your vessel is stout: you have honed her yourself.
Ax, adze, auger. Deck, gunwale, mast: she is whole.
 You culled her from strong ground; her sail is coarse
And spreads like a wing. Her hull is shallow and broad.
 You are made for this; you are the hero, your lifetime
Etched deep — in the grain, in the story before you,
 Like a scar. And you will not sleep. The sea
Still hates you; you are a battleground for spite
 And your beard is a forest of salt. You have spent
The lives of good men like loose coins. The gods
 Have not done with you, but the long years are past!
Your woman is waiting. Your ship is complete.
 You have just begun. Now: Sail.

HUBRIS

In the mouth it
  is a landscape,

the steep slope
  of vowel, the sweep

of lisp, that supple
  horizon, meadow

and cliff. Nearby
  the unlikely light

beating itself
  against the sand.

The sweet field
  unfolds beneath

the man. Vagrant,
  he carries a watery

sack. He is alone
  and perfectly drawn:

his grey rags
  brittle with sea-

salt, his tongue
  carved from stone.

APOSTROPHE

So this is the way
   the stranger comes

to rap at the door
   of your death:

a knucklebone of light
   from behind,

then the dark door
   slamming

and you swim
   the black water.

And it is not
   the swift river

that astounds you,
   but the stranger —

a child, a lightning
   strike, thunder

and diamonds,
   the indifferent face

of steel and bone —
   and that now,

forever, he'll loiter
   at your back,

your soul glittering
   in those eyes.

ON THE DEATH OF PROTEUS

Neither from nor towards.
    — T.S. Eliot, *Four Quartets*

You have wrestled with change
and are not changed. The tide
is and is cast, then recast
on the restless shore —
becoming is being. In the sea
of your changing you are not
washed clean; *humility*
is endless. In the end,
you are everything;
you are already gone.

SOMETIMES THE WHEEL IS ON FIRE[1]

i

Pity in degrees. And the angles of turning:
the permutations never end. We watch the dead

roll by and assume all hell is fury and blame
— so we want for those dead what we want

for ourselves: love and a muted light
to sleep by. We wish them sudden rain

and one great sweetness: respite
from the fire. Then we wish them memory,

a vast catalog of burning; we wish them
their lives all over again. And it is hard

to imagine we grow kind; it is late,
and we have seldom been so. We are turning

ourselves; the ground is slick; we're
moving too fast. And nothing changes.

ii

Yes.
Hard to stumble on the wheel. Turning
ignites turning, and we never stop.

We are as smooth as motionless water,
are as steady as the absence of light

though we burn all our lives: what brightens
our sky starts low and tolerates heaven —

begins and begins again, and the space
between is cinder and flame. We know blame;

we call it fire. And sorrow is a comfort
beyond us. Our hands are bound. Our feet.

We have forgotten our sisters and wives.
We have no sons. And we hear the whispers

of the anxious dead, but we love nothing,
not penitence, not the whorl of blue spark

like a sky. All our days are ruin and smoke.
Forever is deeper than fire. The ground is ash.

No.
Punished. And there are blades beneath
the wheel. We are weary with turning

and dropping down. We watch the saved in the valley
and we burn for that too. And the green hills

are often lit with rain — but want is for
the dying not the dead: nobody listens

and it does not seem to matter:
we are hungry for light, but the fire

is smoking; we are smothered by smoke
but the air feeds the flame. And our daughters

in their bare feet torment us, they scatter us
like hoops, spin us around with their pointed sticks.

Their laughter is like hard wind. And they remind
us of our lives: remorse is not consumed

in fire. We burn with that too; we burn
with everything. The ash is growing deep.

Don't listen.
All love like the wheel. All your life.
And nothing changes despite the fire.

If you turn, you turn alone; your daughters
will not follow. And no one listens.

Blame is made of adamant, of flint, and we fall
over and over like rain. But the river

is flame; memory washes away and the wheel
is unsteady. Don't listen: you can't hear

the rattle or the terrible wind. Can't find
the moving water. And the valley is not

real. We love what comes to us by choice.
We forget the mind rises like heat. Nothing

so sweet, so anxious. And if you do not
love the wheel, you love all that is absent

or in flame. The ground is uncertain
and steep. Sometimes the wheel is on fire.

[1]The title is a footnote to the epigraph, same source.

III

THE REVISIONIST'S DREAM *(III)*

Not that he stole the fire, but that
the body of flame continued there.
And separate, continued — the flame

from the center of the flame,
what fire is. And the dream,
like that too, and the flickering

dance it does. No point: to argue
with the gods in their difficult
clothes, no hope in setting traps

for what we imagine fire to be.
We are all outside the center.
The only way in is to burn.

THE LANGUAGE OF SIRENS
(To a Father)

It runs through the blood, the sweet provocation — the night
you died we could hear it in the blatant lumber of your bones;
everything you said made hard sense. The storm of your leaving
poured
outward, a dark, inviolate sea, and the voice less like a voice
than a song or a wind: you heard it first and it pulled you under.
Love had no say in this. Don't talk to me of love.

Face it: the long sorrow began lifetimes before you loved
a ghost, some shadowy woman, and she left you or died or simply
went away one night,
entered a strange country, or some other world. It's a vague, sad
story; I under-
stand why you never spoke her name. Yet the core of her absent
bones
seemed the source of that hollow whisper: death is a mild specula-
tion. That voice
held you in the palm of its hand; you were dust in its eye. And your
life poured

on, one sadness tumbling from another. Grief swallowed you, it
poured
from you like breath. You wore it like leather and no longer wanted
love —
not a woman or a child — wanted nothing but love's absence and the
insistent voice
that carried like salt breeze over the waves of the liquors you pressed
from night
after night of loneliness. The summer you heard it, within your
child's promising bones,
in her sigh, you understood: the convenient ghost was nothing.
Under

the cover of sorrow your life had taken shape — nothing under
any man's sun changed that. You were made for loneliness. The
    outpour
of heartbreak was wilder than a sea; it flowed around your bones
and the bones of your daughter, it was her own. Beneath her skin it
    shone like love.
And you concealed yourself, hid in the fine mountains, in the bleak
    night
in the cover of disappointment, and she came to you. And the voice

cascaded over the ribs of the forest, wound amidst the rocky
    contours, past the voice-
less, past the blindfolded, deafened others, and under
the pretense of love you built the fire. Each night
it raged — you thought it would save you — but the flames poured
out, the staves of your frail body washed in burning. Only the song
    survived. And love,
passed down like the configuration of the body, gathered like the
    bone-

dry kindling, rife with promise fleeting as your own spent bones,
is shallow in the wake of such singing. And this is what you leave
    behind: a voice,
a confirmation — the confluence of lives — the careful measure, the
    paucity of love
in the singular awareness: you are always alone. You must have
    under-
stood even then. And still your breath pours
from her like wind — one darkness to another, her nights

riddled with the trill of the unfaltering breeze in your transient bones.
    Under
those lightless skies, in her quick blood, the voice is a constant
    pouring
forth, a storm, much like an absent love, in the longest, empty night.

THE EMBERS, THE LIGHT

Regret must be colored
      like this: the sky
grey as dust, the rim low

      and fat with shadow —
then above you it catches
      slowly: one star,

a moon, yellow fire
      over the reservoir.
You are a pinprick

      of sterner dark,
the locus of sorrow.
      You keep your head

down, insist,
      without relenting,
you are as blind

      as dirt —
the embers, the light,
      are nothing, mean less.

THAT FALL: ICARUS IN THE EXURBS

No matter how I plot that fall,
    I'm obliged to call it flight:
that next-to-the-top unblemished step,
    the oaks like blithe sky, the moist
yellow sun, its poultice heat, and the arc
    so majestic you would have named it
bitter wind or *wingèd body coming forth*
    — the beauty of the journey,
trajectory of the gods, the faultless entry
    to the gravel sea: shoulder, neck,
elbow, knee. And the stunned stillness
    of the woman at the bottom,
grateful, blessed, still breathing.

LETTER TO A HUSBAND

Dear X,

      You mistake my sadness: we are *all* rowing in the dark.
   Incident
is moot — the long haul matters. And how we see it: the waves
    drinking
us in, the enormous emptiness of sky and that tide we call love. No
   one
drowns in loving; we can live with doubt and the narrow
span of oars. But we want the sea placid, and its depth, its absolute
    darkness,
contained — we are not swimmers, not built for epic gestures. Our
    arms

are weak, and we long for the company of dogs, the dense green
    forest, its armature
of pine and oak. We'd like solid footing. We would pass whole lives
    without incident
if we could. And we will leave so much unsaid. We are already
    lonely. Our natures are dark
and lazy; our vices will be our undoing — we are given to drink
and selfishness. To silence. We are divided like that, and we borrow
unhappiness — our catalog of pasts, the endless lists of error, one

indistinguishable from the next, a rapid blur of omission and miscal-
culation, every one
ripe with ghosts we love to repent of, each replete with longings, with
armies
of poor choices roiling about us like banners, their arrows
dipped in regret. A person could drown in regret, a constant, inciden-
tal
danger of rowing. But the charms of the water are strong, and we
drink,
eager and anxious, the impossible and the past. And what comes for
us in the dark

is how we measure our happiness. We are such seers in the darkness
that swims behind us! It's the *would be* and the *might*, not the *was*
that sets us one
against the other, that squats in the foreground of each luminous
noon and dazzles us into drink,
that leaves us blind and listening to ghosts. We could disarm
those shades; we could shake them from our eyes and from our
tongues — and praise coincidence,
the happenstance that brought us here, together. We could outgrow

the cargo of weariness that would let us drown, set the past free to
row
its own black way. We could settle for the sound of the sea in the
distance, the dark
waves slapping behind us. We would still be free to fail. It's no
coincidence —
the shore is a shifty, ambivalent margin: it leads to the sea, leads to
our woods, as well. And everyone
knows the tide is ongoing, contrary, is a rising and falling thing. But
we're armed
for inconsistency! Let's lean back, drowse at the oarlocks, drink

the bright liquor of *is* and *are*. In the discernible distance, we could
conjure up a sun to drink
our worry. Anticipation needn't be so dim. In all our harried rowing,
we failed to raise our eyes! We took the sky for nothing, for granted,
our arms
fixed to the oars, our gaze on the changeable water. We have been
blind and blamed the darkness
while overhead stars grazed amidst the consequential orbits and one
by one they lit the sky, each bright point an incidence

of significant fire, a meeting of singular light drinking up the stub-
born dark. When we choose
to row, if we choose to see, they might flicker along our consequent
waves — one might burn
an arm's length away, one star on the water so bright, the dark will be
incidental, and we will shine.

WHAT WE DON'T UNDERSTAND

looks up at us and begs. It sits up. Bends
its outstretched paws at what would be the wrists —

we think it looks like us, or something like us,
but...different somehow. It has a tail. And there's

something in the eyes, something deep. But it wears
strange clothes: a collar, thick fur. And it knows

we're lost, we haven't got a clue. Wouldn't know one
if we saw one. And it's true, we don't, we wouldn't.

But its tail thumps like our poor hearts beating
and what we don't understand welcomes us home,

gives out its message in sharp, nearly comprehensible
bursts. We love that. And we bark back, our blunt

tongues wagging. We think what we don't know
loves us, but we can't even call it by name.

So we give it a name. It's mysterious. And for all
we know we might be saying *footstool, pig's eye,*

or *rich black dirt.* We'll never be sure. But we
go on. And we brag; we write long, painful essays

on our progress. Others read them. But what we really
understand is this: we want. And what we don't comprehend

is unfathomable. What we hear is the wind
and our own fears rumbling. But we could

be mistaken. We are often mistaken
and so little is visible — for instance,

the wind and what we do not know.
What we don't understand. What sounds

like it might be our home — unknowable wind
and the black, thumping heart of the world.

Photo: Noni Diamantopoulos

ABOUT THE AUTHOR

Renée Ashley's books include SALT (Brittingham Prize in Poetry, University of Wisconsin Press, 1991) and THE VARIOUS REASONS OF LIGHT (Avocet Press Inc, 1998). She has received awards from the Poetry Society of America, and the KENYON REVIEW (from which she has been awarded both the Award for Emerging Writers and the Award for Literary Excellence), along with the CHELSEA Award in Poetry, the AMERICAN LITERARY REVIEW Award in Poetry, The Charles Angoff Award from THE LITERARY REVIEW, and a Pushcart Prize. She has been the recipient of fellowships from the New Jersey State Council on the Arts and the National Endowment for the Arts. She is Assistant Poetry Coordinator for the Geraldine R. Dodge Foundation.